Praise for
7 Steps to Spiritual Empathy

"In the midst of today's hectic pace of life this beautifully written book thoughtfully reminds us that first and foremost, we are relational beings. It is through relating and within relationship that we find meaning in our lives.

Jenny's insightful and yet pragmatic approach to greater emotional awareness awakens us to the love that is possible in each moment we share with others. This book is overflowing with kindness, insight, depth and above all...love."

Katherine Woodward Thomas,
New York Times Bestselling Author of Calling in "The One"

"I absolutely love this book! It is an amazing resource written in such an accessible way.

It's a joy to read a book that reminds us that we are relational beings. By relating to ourselves and noticing our core experience Jenny reminds us of the power and choice this gives us. An important read for all"

Dr Laura Hill,
Counselling Psychologist, BPS Chartered HCPC Accredited

This book has been a delight to read and has given some real structure to an exploration of emotions.

When working with people either as a coach, a supervisor, manager or colleague I frequently ask a question which is "What do you know about yourself?"

The book will be an invaluable resource and support a gentler journey for those I work with, and for myself. I love the language of kindness and responsibility. It may also lend itself to an extended period, not just the days as recommended by Jenny.

The added link to the podcast session is a wonderful bonus which supports todays expectation of digital/virtual resource and activity.

In the context of what feels like a divided United Kingdom I think this is recommended reading for anyone trying to understand their own and others reactions and to seek a way forward.

**Libby Alderson,
Chartered Fellow CIPD. Coach & Organisational Coach
Supervisor**

"A beautifully written book that will be an invaluable resource for anyone interested in learning more about themselves. I particularly like her daily 'invitations'. Jenny's book is accessible, practical and inspiring."

Juliet Grayson, Psychotherapist and Author of Landscapes of the Heart: the working world of a sex and relationship therapist

"Amidst an ever-increasingly frantic world, Jenny's book offers an insightful, accessible and pragmatic guide to anyone who wishes to develop their emotional intelligence and self-compassion. In my opinion, these qualities form the bedrock for the possibility of living a fulfilling and happy life."

Wendy Bramham, MBACP (Snr Accred) WPF BA (Hons)
Psychotherapist, Counselling Supervisor, Executive Coach

Jenny's book gives us all an easy to follow guide for reaching those long sought-after goals of giving our lives a deeper meaning.

Whilst Jenny advocates it as being a book you can read in seven days, each of Jenny sentences is so packed with good solid understanding that it is too good to read to put down again so quickly!

I am sure I shall use my copy is more of a handbook that I shall continually returned to, to help me continue my journey seeking that place of perfect empathy balance and space.

Edd Edgell
Independent Therapist and Supervisor

Jenny Florence guides us gently and skilfully through the seven stages of knowing our capacity for self-empathy. There is much wisdom in this short book which teaches us the delicate art of mindful self-care in the service of relationship, with the promise of a better world for us all as a result.

Tom Corbishley.
MCCP psychotherapist

7 Steps to Spiritual Empathy
a practical guide

The Spiritual Philosophy of Emotional Intelligence

The first in the series of books
"The Intelligence of Our Emotions"

by
Jenny Florence

7 Steps to Spiritual Empathy

A Practical Guide

First Published 2016 A-Z of Emotional Health

Copyright © Jenny Florence/J L Burgess 2016

Cover Image Zen White Spa Stones, Twindesigner, courtesy of Pond 5

ISBN 978-0-9955079-0-6

Additional Recourses to Support your Journey.

Free Worksheets to accompany this book are available to Download with your free meditation "The Transformational Power of Emotion."

Download at www.spiritualempathy.com/meditation/

Jenny also offers readers the opportunity to receive updates about Free Audios and Free Meditations. If this is of interest to you, please register your details on her homepage.

www.jennyflorencehealth.com

A 7 Day Series of Meditations based on this book can be accessed through Jenny's on-line Audio Library.

www.a-z-of-emotionalhealth.com

7 Steps to Spiritual Empathy, a Practical Guide

Dedication

"None of us got to where we are alone.

Whether the assistance we received was obvious or subtle, acknowledging someone's help is a big part of understanding the importance of saying thank you."

Harvey Mackay

Born 1932. Business Man.

I am continually in awe of our human capacity to grow beyond that which has caused, and indeed may still be causing us difficulty.

This book is dedicated to the extraordinary people who I have had the privilege to work with over many years.

You have found the courage to walk through my door and to invite me to walk alongside you for a part of your journey. You have shared your vulnerabilities and your struggles, your fears and your disappointments. You have shared your learning curves, your growths, your successes and allowed me to be witness to the emergence, evolution and fruition of new hopes and new dreams.

You have shown me time and again that when we truly desire change, regardless of where we have come from, and regardless of what may have taken place in our lives, when we learn to listen to life through Empathy, indeed when we learn to live life through Empathy, the landscape of our world, both inner and outer, will change.

A personal thank you also goes to Sue, for her unswerving faith in my ability to write and to James whose keen eye and objective editorial feedback has enabled this book to be as you find it today.

"When you start to develop your powers of empathy and imagination, the whole world opens up to you."

Susan Sarandon

Born 1946. Actress.

Contents

7 Steps to Spiritual Empathy, a Practical Guide

7 Steps to Spiritual Empathy, a Practical Guide

How to use this Book
"Walking with Empathy"

"We are not human beings having a spiritual experience. We are spiritual beings having a human experience."

Pierre Teilhard de Chardin.

Born 1881. French Philosopher, Jesuit Priest.

S o how best can you use this book, or perhaps I should say how best can you engage and relate with this book?

The next seven chapters are designed to be read daily, exploring what I have come to refer to as the seven principles of spiritual empathy. I use my words here thoughtfully, and spiritual, is a word consciously chosen.

Worksheets for journaling to support your journey are available to download from www.spiritualempathy.com/meditation/ with the free meditation download that comes as a gift with this book.

Over the next seven days and in the next seven chapters we are going to fully embrace and dance with the true nature of empathy, in all of its glory. We are going to embark on a journey of emotional and spiritual curiosity, each day opening a deepening avenue of thought and experience.

I fully acknowledge that for some of us, the personal meaning and significance of our spirituality will sit in direct relationship with a particular faith, however, within this book I do not use this word in any specific religious context.

I am deeply respectful of anyone's individual beliefs however, within this book, I am talking about spirituality as a way of life. Something that we are, as much as something that we either say or do. And if I have a wish within these pages, it is a desire for our journey together to be a journey of deepening intimacy with empathy in ways that enable our experience of our real everyday living to become more enriched and more alive.

To navigate our lives from a position of meaning, we will need to be emotionally available as well as mentally available.

When we consider intellectual and spiritual concepts, if they remain a principle in thought, rather than a lived and real experience that is **"felt"**, then we create a kind of disconnect. A disconnection between the way that we think about our lives, and the way that we actually experience and therefore live our lives; and this is actually contrary to everything that empathy is, and everything that empathy offers us, in the enhancement of the daily quality of our lives.

I suppose in short, in order to truly thrive and to flourish, we will need to be able to integrate intellectual and spiritual concepts in ways that connect to our real experience of what it is to be fully human and fully alive; and we will need to be able to integrate intellectual and spiritual concepts in ways that we can consciously manifest within the reality of our daily lives.

We will need to experience ourselves and others with meaning. We will need to experience life itself with meaning. Thinking, saying, and doing will need to integrate and become one with us. We will need to walk our talk and it is empathy that gifts us with this possibility.

As we explore and develop our understanding of the seven principles of spiritual empathy as a state of being, each chapter then concludes with an

14

invitation for the day, with thoughts and suggestions as to how each principle might be integrated into our real experience of daily living.

"Suffering ceases to be suffering at the moment it finds a meaning."

Viktor E. Frankl.

Born 1905. Neurologist, Psychiatrist, Holocaust Survivor.

7 Steps to Spiritual Empathy, a Practical Guide

Introduction

"The Dynamic and Transformational Power
of Empathy"

"We live in a universe of dynamic fields of energy, a dynamic universe that includes ourselves. We are intricate energy systems, fields transcending our physical bodies and reaching out to touch and influence other energy systems."

James Redfield.

Born 1950. Author of The Celestine Prophecy, Lecturer, Screenwriter & Film Producer.

Are you interested in the power of conscious choice?

Do you understand the role that your emotions play in your capacity for conscious living?

Do you feel as though you are in charge of the decisions that you make in your life; in charge of navigating your own journey?

We are becoming increasingly aware of the power and influence of our extraordinary mind in co-creating our journey throughout our lives and there are numerous books and numerous scientific studies that are connecting both the science and the spirituality of energy, and indeed our human capacity for conscious choice and influence within this sphere. However, our mind is only one part of the picture; it is only one piece of the jigsaw.

It has been my privilege to walk alongside literally hundreds of people as they have journeyed from the chaos of living from an emotionally reactive position, to a place of integrated living where their emotions fuel and feed their capacity to navigate their lives from a position of conscious, reflective choice. Indeed, the journey of my own life has shown me through and through, that our emotions play an absolutely integral role in our ability to heal, to grow and to thrive.

If you are interested in deepening your emotional awareness and in developing your emotional intelligence in ways that enhance conscious co-creative living, then this book is for you.

This book is designed to be read in 7 days, with approximately 10 minutes of reading each day.

If as adults we are the author of our own experience, then how do we become fully present and fully available to navigate our journey through life with conscious intention?

How do we find ways that will enable us to be actively and consciously co-creative, mindful of our choices and indeed mindful of the consequences of our choices?

The answer is Empathy.

Empathy isn't simply a listening ear and something that we can offer others. In essence, true empathy is a state of being. When we live empathically, we can relate with our full experience of life at a level of mindful and conscious awareness. Awareness of ourselves, awareness of others, and awareness of a greater, universal intelligence of which we are an integral and dynamic part.

Empathy is the very fabric of relatedness.

Living through empathy **IS** living through relationship. It is about being fully relational, and fully present to our entire experience. When we engage with life through empathy we create a relational connection with life itself.

"I've worked all my life on the subject of awareness, whether it's awareness of the body, awareness of the mind, awareness of your emotions, awareness of your relationships, or awareness of your environment.

I think the key to transforming your life is to be aware of who you are."

Deepak Chopra.

Born 1947. Author, Philosopher, Public Speaker, Alternative Medicine Advocate.

Chapter 1

The First Principle of True Empathy
"The Space Within"

"Thirty spokes share the wheels hub; it is the centre hole that makes it useful.

Shape clay into a vessel; it is the space within that makes it useful.

Cut doors and Windows for a room; it is the holes which make it useful.

Therefore profit comes from what is there; usefulness from what is not there."

Lao Tse.

531 BC. Chinese Philosopher and Writer, Founder of Philosophical Taoism.

When I was just 16 years old I picked up the Tao te Ching, the book opened, and I read the passage above. I have never forgotten it, and whenever I think about true empathy, I am always reminded of these words.

The first principle of empathy is actually about creating space; creating a space where we listen and we hear, without preconception and without judgement. When someone relates to us with true empathy, they offer us a space in which we can literally **"be"**; a space where we feel safe enough to be fully present and safe enough to be heard. And regardless of the way that we are feeling, we feel welcomed and received.

To be truly empathic we are creating a space and we are "holding" that space safely.

So what do I mean by "holding"? What "holds" a space?

A structure or a boundary that creates and maintains an empathic space may or may not be visible. In some instances, there may be some physical parameters, a room or house that feels safe, or its structure may in part be constructed through words, like a verbal contract or agreement; but most importantly, it will be made up of the substance of qualities, such as consistency, reliability, acceptance, interest and appreciation, and each of these qualities contribute and make up the dynamic substance of trust.

When we **"hold space"** we not only keep these qualities and values in mind, but we also **"hold"** them in our actions. Our awareness stretches beyond an intellectual or moral concept. Our awareness stretches beyond our seeing, beyond our listening, and beyond an understanding. When we hold space, our awareness has become integrated into doing, and integrated into being.

Through action, the qualities and substance of trust have become integrated into our own dynamic field of energy with a mindful awareness of conscious decision and conscious choice both to ourselves as well as to others. This is Empathy.

In effect, when we offer a space of **"holding"** to another, our presence and our actions create both the boundary as well as the container.

When I meet someone for the first time in my therapeutic practice, I often say to them that trust is something that we will need to discover. I can talk about confidentiality and tell them that the therapeutic environment that I offer is a safe space where they can speak about anything that they need to. **However, in truth, trust is not something that we can simply**

22

say, it is something that we do. And for real trust to emerge, they will need to come to know me. They will need to have a real experience of what it is like to sit with me; a real experience of what it is like to **"Be"** with me.

To be fully emotionally present and to be able to presence ourselves with true authenticity; to share our vulnerabilities, our strengths and our weaknesses and our mistakes as well as our successes, we need to feel safe. We need to know that our feelings and emotions as well as our thoughts, will be received and welcomed, listened to and heard.

To experience safety and to develop trust we will need parameters and boundaries that create a space of "holding". A lack of boundaries can feel emotionally frightening, and potentially overwhelming.

So true empathy embodies a harmonious balance of both structure and space.

Regardless of whether it is visible to the naked eye or not, a structure is present; a profitable and valuable structure. A structure which, by its very nature creates a definition of trust and safety, in which the space of usefulness or possibility can take place.

Now the substance of a structure, or a boundary, is very important. Just as the shape of a structure will define the shape of the space within, the substance of the structure or the boundaries, will become the nature, or the defining quality, of the space within.

A boundary or a limit that has been forced upon us or generated through the misuse of power, will feel oppressive. It is made of the substance of fear. Any boundary built in fear, even if we created it ourselves on the basis of self-preservation, will be about control, a reaction to a fear of being out of control. These kinds of structures are inevitably rigid and inflexible and create limitations that stifle growth and opportunity.

Whereas, boundaries that are created through mutuality, respect, interest and compassion, are aspects of love. Even though these boundaries are strong, solid and firm, they are also flexible at the same time. They create a dynamic space that is full of movement, potential growth and opportunity.

Space and boundaries are working harmoniously together. They are in relationship, and this relationship becomes the stage for emotional expression and mindful contemplation.

When we listen to our lives through our logical thinking, we are living through the intelligence of our mind. When we listen to our lives through our emotions, we are living through the intelligence of our heart. We need both, not one at the expense of the other, and empathy sits at the very core of our ability to engage with life from both our heart, as well as our mind.

When we create an empathic space within, we create a **"holding ground"** where our mind and our emotions can work in harmony together.

Our emotions can serve their true purpose. Like an internal satnav system, they bring us vital information, and this in collaboration with our extraordinary mind fuels informative decision-making, enabling us to embrace choice and to navigate our lives with compassion and meaning.

Our mind and our emotions are an extraordinary team and the very fabric of this extraordinary union is bound together by Empathy. The presence of our emotional voice in collaboration with reflective, considered thought, sows seeds of possibility and open doorways of opportunity for change and for natural evolutionary growth.

When the intelligence of our mind dances with the intelligence of our heart we become present and available to be fully engaged in conscious creative living.

My Thought for Today

My Mind and My Emotions Hold Space for Possibility

My Invitation

Today I wish to invite you to deepen your understanding of what it is to "hold space", and primarily, to develop your ability to "hold space" for yourself.

My Thoughts and Suggestions

Consider making today a day of noticing.

Our first task in developing any kind of evolving and deepening awareness is to notice. So today I wish to invite you to develop your capacity to notice and to become aware of your own internal space within. A holding space within, in which your thinking mind can meet with your emotional experience.

At least three times today, consider taking time to pause.

And as you pause for a moment, bring your attention to yourself. Notice what you are thinking in this present moment. Notice what you are feeling in this present moment, and become aware of any specific emotions that are present. Also notice any particular sensations in your physical body. Are you relaxed? Are you tense? Where in your body are you feeling this?

Now ask yourself these questions?

- Were you aware of these experiences or have they only come to your attention because you paused and took time to notice?
- Does your mind meet with your experiences with an openness, with enquiry and interest, or does the noticing of your thoughts and your emotions generate further thinking that may hold

critical or negative perceptions? Does an inner critic occupy your space within?

- How easily are you able to identify your different emotions. Is your mind familiar with the different emotional states that you may be feeling? Many of us haven't been brought up with a fluent emotional language, and this isn't because our parents didn't want to give us one, but simply because they were not brought up to be emotionally fluent themselves. (1)
- Do you think that you would be more receptive to experiencing the thoughts and emotions of another, than the thoughts and emotions of yourself? It's fascinating how many people will offer empathy to others and yet rarely pause to take the time to listen to themselves.

This exercise is purely one of noticing.

It is an interesting exercise because it helps us to become more mindful of whether our internal space within is open and available for the holding and processing of our real here and now experience, or whether it is busy and full of clutter.

It also helps us to identify whether the boundaries around our internal space contain anxiety, criticism, or any elements of fear and control.

It also helps us to identify whether there is a difference between our availability for ourselves and our availability for others.

It is fair to say that very few of us will be able to do an exercise like this and come away from it feeling as though we were fully available and fully present to our experiences, however, the key to initiating any kind of change is to first begin to notice, and our desire today is simply to bring to our attention the value of noticing.

When we notice, we immediately create the possibility of observing our own experience. We can notice and gently challenge any judgements held in our mind and encourage the arrival of experience with interest, with enquiry and with a desire to understand.

When we "hold" space, we "hold" this possibility.

"The self must know stillness before it can discover its true song."

Ralph Blum.

Born 1932. Author of the Book of Runes.

1 Our understanding of the benefits and need for emotional literacy are a relatively recent development. For further reading in this area I would suggest authors such as Daniel Goleman, author of "Emotional Intelligence" and Karla McLaren, author of "The Language of Emotions".

7 Steps to Spiritual Empathy, a Practical Guide

Chapter 2

The Second Principle of Empathy

"To Receive"

The Guest House

"This being human is a guest house. Every morning a new arrival.

A joy, a depression, a meanness, some momentary awareness comes as an unexpected visitor.

Welcome and entertain them all!

Even if they're a crowd of sorrows, who violently sweep your house, empty of its furniture,

still treat each guest honourably.

He may be clearing you out for some new delight.

The dark thought, the shame, the malice, meet them at the door laughing, and invite them in.

Be grateful for whoever comes, because each has been sent as a guide from beyond."

Rumi.

Born 1207. Persian Poet.

We tend to think about empathy as our ability to receive the emotional experiences of others, however, in truth, if we are unable to create an internal space of empathy for ourselves, we will be unable to create a fully available internal space of empathy to receive others.

Whether it is in relationship to others, or whether it is in relationship to ourselves, the empathic space within is the same space.

This space within, this unseen space, held within unseen boundaries, is the landing ground where experience arrives. A kind of melting pot where our experience of life including our emotional experience will arrive and be interpreted by our mind.

Our emotions are an extraordinary gift. Our emotions, our feelings, are our navigational system and it's an extraordinary system.

Our emotions give us information; they are the ultimate relational tool. They are ultra-responsive and very immediate. If you think about it, the way that we feel, can change in an instant, and this is actually one of the ways in which our emotions serve us. They are literally giving us minute by minute information, all of the time. And not only are they letting us know how we feel about whatever's going on in the world around us, they are also letting us know how we feel deep down inside of ourselves.

If our mind is unable to receive and to listen to this emotional information with welcome, interest and compassion, then not only will we have difficulty in engaging with our own here and now, real experience, but we will also struggle to interpret the emotional experiences of others.

The perceptions of our mind colour the way in which we perceive the feelings and moods of both ourselves as well as the feelings and moods of those around us.

If we have learned to be afraid of our emotions, particularly those that tend to be labelled as negative or bad, then rather than welcoming our emotions, our mind can perceive them as a kind of enemy, an enemy within. And when this happens, our mind can develop complex strategies to defend against the way that we feel.

Rather than engaging in relationship with our emotions, our mind becomes actively involved in trying to keep our emotions under control. The unseen boundaries that support, shape and contain the unseen empathic space within, become controlling and restrictive, driven by fear.

Emotions arrive regardless, but they are neither welcomed nor received, and as unwelcome guests, they remain unheard, unprocessed, and unresolved.

The space within becomes cluttered, full of unprocessed emotional content and full of emotional history; like a holding ground for unresolved emotional expression. The stage for emotional expression and collaborative transformation is fully occupied, spilling over at the edges and there is little or no room to receive and consider new information with clarity, from either ourselves, or from others, and this sits in the way of being able to engage with our real experience, right here, and right now.

When we understand that our emotions are vital and valuable, when we challenge any misinformed perspectives of our mind, and we welcome and receive our emotions, with interest, respect and compassion, the nature of the unseen boundaries immediately changes, and in turn, the very nature of the space within also changes.

As our emotions are welcomed and received, processed and released, and as they take centre stage in their transformational role; a previously rigid and inflexible space of unnecessary restriction, becomes a dynamic space, flexible and open to growth and to learning and we can engage fully in relationship with our real experience, right here and right now. The energetic field within us and around us becomes open and available for conscious intention and conscious choice.

Wisdom is the creative outcome of knowledge and experience integrating and joining together. And it is our emotional experience combined with the knowledge of our mind that enables this to happen.

In our adult lives, the meeting of our mind and our emotions is one of the most influential relationships we will ever have and the quality of the relationship and the communication between them lays the foundation for a partnership that is fluent in navigating experience.

When intention sits in thought alone, it is disconnected from our extraordinary human capacity to be fully immersed in life itself and therefore disconnected from our capacity as human beings to be fully transformational.

As we develop empathy, we develop a thriving relationship between our mind, and our emotions. A relationship in which the intelligence of our heart, unites in equal partnership with the intelligence of our mind. A relationship where conscious thought sits in harmony with the power of emotional feeling.

Connectedness does not exist solely in the mind. Connectedness is a fully integrated experience.

Intention and co-creativity are not simply about thought. Life is about **being**, and **being** is a connectedness, a relatedness, with life itself.

My Thought for Today

I Open My Mind to Welcome and Receive All of My Emotions.

My Invitation

Today I wish to invite you to notice and where necessary, consider re-framing your perception of your emotions.

All of our emotions are absolutely vital to us. Whether we are feeling immensely joyous or desperately unhappy our emotions are bringing us good information. Even the most challenging of our emotions are informing us. These difficult feelings are letting us know, in no uncertain terms, that something is wrong.

To be fully available to navigate our lives with conscious intention, we need to be fully available to receive our entire experience of what it is to be alive. We need to be able to receive our entire experience in order to be, a human **"being"**.

My Thoughts and Suggestions

Let us first bring to mind the value of noticing. The starting point of any kind of conscious change is to notice and to become aware.

At least three times today consider making time to pause.

Bring your attention to yourself and become aware of both your thoughts and your emotions.

Notice the quality of the relationship that you have with your emotions. Do you consider them to be friends? Are they welcome guests?

How does your mind perceive your emotions? Is your mind judgemental of your emotions, critical or dismissive or is your mind interested, supportive and encouraging of your feelings?

7 Steps to Spiritual Empathy, a Practical Guide

Is your mind inclined to have an internal dialogue **"about"** them? Or is your mind in conversation **"with"** them? When we are talked **"about"**, we are not involved in the discussion and at the mercy of perception, however, when we are spoken **"with"**, we are an active participant within the conversation. Notice and become aware of this difference.

Take a piece of paper and draw a line down the middle, from top to bottom. On one side write down the way that you feel about a situation and list your emotions. On the other side, list the way that your mind perceives these emotions.

Ask your mind to notice your feelings and ask your mind to listen. What are your emotions trying to tell you?

We often tend to classify emotions in very black and white terms. The positive and the negative, the good or the bad. This language is a rigid and inflexible description and doesn't afford us the opportunity to receive the information that our emotions bring us with a mindful receptivity. This kind of classification can generate fear and anxiety, particularly if we don't understand why we are feeling the way that we are.

Your emotions are the bringers of information, and this information needs to be welcomed and received by your mind.

If you do not feel ok then something is needing to be addressed. Whether you need to take time for yourself, or whether you need support from a friend, a family member, or indeed whether you need some kind of professional support, however challenging, your emotions are trying to bring something to your attention, and this is good information.

Noticing will always be the first step in being able to create change.

When our mind is open to noticing our emotional experience with interest and without judgement, the empathic space within becomes available to receive, not only our own experience but the experiences of others. This in turn creates opportunity for conscious decision making and conscious choice.

"An inability to notice our true feelings leaves us at their mercy."

Daniel Goleman.

Born 1946. Author of Emotional Intelligence, Psychologist, Science Journalist.

7 Steps to Spiritual Empathy, a Practical Guide

Chapter 3

The Third Principle of Empathy

"Reflection"

"Anytime new insight replaces an old assumption or a fossilized perception is the spring. New understandings sprout, new tolerances appear, and new curiosity draws you to previously dark places. Just as the sun shines earlier and longer in the spring, changes that seemed impossible appear to be possible with each new insight."

Gary Zukav.

Born 1942. Author of The Seat of the Soul, Spiritual Teacher.

As we journey with empathy, we have created a space of welcome and set the stage for emotional expression to be received, a stage where the intelligence of our heart sits in an equal and dynamic relationship with the intelligence of our mind.

Welcome to the third principle in the true nature of empathy. Reflection.

True reflection sits in a state of paradox.

True reflection involves an ability to be both present, and yet an observer at the same time. To sit in a space of true reflection we will need to be fully available to both participate in the space and experience the content, and yet at the same time not fully occupy this space. Our capacity to be truly reflective, will be relative to our ability to be involved, and yet un-involved in the same moment.

One of the tools often used to develop our empathy in relation to others is to consider how we might feel if we were standing in the other person's shoes. This is a wonderful tool, however, if we become overly identified with their story, then our perception of the way that they feel, has the potential to be coloured too much by our own history and our own experiences. Too much of our own experience is occupying the space and this will colour our perceptions.

Whether we are listening to ourselves or to others, objectivity plays a vital role in our capacity for truly reflective thought.

If we are offering a space of empathic availability to someone else, it is very important to check out and to enquire, and to take the time to discover how the other person actually thinks and feels about their situation. We need to take the time to discover and find out how the other person is perceiving and experiencing their situation first hand.

Likewise, if we are listening to ourselves it is vital that we free ourselves from any loaded preconception or assumptions and take time to really hear and consider all aspects of our experience.

So the art of being empathic lies in our capacity to be fully engaged, and yet disengaged at the same time. We need to be able to identify and yet remain unidentified at the same time; to be deeply involved and to care and yet hold an objective position.

In this way, the space within retains its capacity for full receptivity as well as its potential for objective thought.

True reflection involves both our mind and our emotions. We listen to the way that we are feeling and we listen to our thoughts. True reflection is a flowing relationship in which our mind and our emotions unite in relatedness and engage in a dance together.

The space within is both a space of welcome and a space of emotional safety, and yet is also a space of curiosity and interest with the potential for serious and challenging thought and consideration, as well as playfulness and creativity.

When we occupy a space of reflection we sit in paradox because as a space of learning and possibility it is by its very nature a place of movement and potential growth, and yet it is also a place of stillness, peacefulness and quiet.

Reflection is never a busy place.

When we offer empathy to others, we offer invitation, with welcome, with interest and with compassion. The very nature of being present to someone else's story means that in some way we will become a participant in their story and an actor in their play, even if only for a short while.

By choosing to share their story with us, they in turn offer us an invitation; an invitation to be both a participant, as well as their audience, at that moment in time. And as an independent observer, receiving them with welcome, curiosity and interest, we can become a mirror to their experience, a mirror to their story, a mirror that enables them to receive themselves with interest, compassion and with a greater impartiality.

When we offer empathy to ourselves, we open an invitation to look inwards. The space within literally becomes a space of in-sight, a space of inner vision and inner reflection. A space where we become an observer of our own experience, whilst at the same time, a participant in our own experience.

We are the tellers of our story and we are the actors in our play. We are the audience and we are the writer of the script.

When we bear witness to our own story, having an internal space of reflection and inner vision creates the opportunity for us to make considered changes in the scripts that we are writing. With conscious intention we can make considered changes in the scripts of our own life story.

Embracing true reflection is a one of the most valuable tools that we have available to us. It enables us to notice. Being able to notice will always be the first step in being able to actively create conscious change. In noticing any patterns of behaviour or emotionally laden reactions that are taking centre stage in our journey we create the opportunity to let go of any repeating or reoccurring history.

Embracing true reflection as part of our daily living, supports us in living from a position of a continual deepening awareness, keeping the space within free flowing and free of clutter and noise.

Embracing true reflection creates opportunity and availability for conscious choice and conscious intention.

My Thought for Today

True Reflection Creates Opportunity for Conscious Choice.

My Invitation

Today I wish to invite you to consciously create a space in your day for reflection.

My Thoughts and Suggestions

Ideally at the end of your day I wish to invite you to make space to cast your mind back through your waking hours. Allow yourself to recall and to notice different aspects of your experience throughout the day.

Do you tend to remember and to dwell on the challenging moments or on the more joyous ones?

Invite yourself to acknowledge and validate your achievements as well as any situations that retrospectively, you would have liked to have been different.

If you find yourself remembering any kinds of challenging experience, invite your mind to journey back to that moment in time. Stand back and look at the scene laid out before you. Consider the situation and anyone involved. Take your time.

What you were thinking about and feeling at that time? What kinds of emotions were present? How do you both think and feel about this right now?

We cannot be in charge of the actions of others, however, we can take charge of our own capacity for conscious choice. When we can see ourselves as the source of potential change, and know that we ourselves contain the seeds of possibility we can begin to take some time to consider what we could have done differently.

7 Steps to Spiritual Empathy, a Practical Guide

If you find yourself approaching this exercise with any kind of self-criticism or judgement, bear in mind that self-criticism sits within us for all kinds of reasons. If we begin to notice that we have a significant inner critic, then this in itself is deserving of our attention, with compassion and with care.

Something that I have come across on many occasions with people who have a raging inner critic, is that when they begin to notice their inner critical voice, rather than viewing their increasing capacity to notice themselves as a significant step in creating change, they view the reoccurrence of this habitual inner voice as some kind of failure and they then begin to criticise themselves for being critical!

Please don't do this.

Reflection involves making time and space for our mind and our emotions to engage in an influential and collaborative relationship resulting in conscious and meaningful choice.

When we take time to notice and to reflect on how something might have been different, we are engaging in a process of learning that actively creates retrospective wisdom.

When we take time to receive our experiences and to reflect, without preconception and without judgement, we can begin to see both ourselves and others through different eyes.

"The real voyages of Discovery consist not in seeking new landscapes but in having new eyes."

Marcel Proust.

Born 1871. Novelist.

Chapter 4

The Fourth Principle of Empathy

"Respect"

"We must say "no" to what, in our heart, we don't want. We must say "no" to doing things out of

obligation, thereby cheating those important to us of the purest expression of our love."

Suzette Hinton.

Author, Innovator, Founder of Statistics be Darned.

Welcome to the fourth principle of empathy, **Respect**. In the first principle of empathy, "the Space Within", I spoke about the relationship and between space and boundaries.

Respect is a boundary.

Respect creates a boundary that recognizes and validates our individuality whilst simultaneously acknowledging and recognizing the validity of others.

Respect shapes the energetic field both within us and around us and in doing so affords us the opportunity to be witness to any differences between ourselves and others without judgement. Respect creates an energetic field of mutuality, where despite our differences, we share a common desire for understanding.

Even though we cannot see it, respect is something that we can feel. It is a tangible and yet unseen experience. Hopefully most of us will know what it feels like to be treated with respect, even when faced with a difference of opinion, however, I suspect, with sadness, that most of us will also know what it feels like to be on the receiving end of a lack of respect or an inability on the part of another to consider our thoughts and opinions as valid, regardless of agreement.

Like many qualities, respect can be open to misrepresentation and manipulation. I have come across instances where respect is a word that is used in a way that I would consider to be inappropriate.

Someone once told me that they respected their father, when in fact as our conversation emerged it became apparent that they feared their father.

Respect born of fear is not true respect.

True respect creates a boundary that denotes care and regard, a boundary that symbolises the health and well-being of our own sense of entitlement, as well as our recognition and desire to support and validate the entitlement of others.

True respect acknowledges and validates the differences between us and therefore our unique individuality, indeed true respect celebrates difference. If we consider that a boundary or a structure defines the nature of the space within, then respect creates the quality of a space in which difference is welcomed as an opportunity for discovery, for learning, and therefore for growth.

So true respect creates definition within relationship. A space where both similarity and disagreement can be validated; a space where agreements can be discussed, negotiated and made, even if those agreements are in celebration of a difference of opinion.

True respect, acknowledges and validates our right and our opportunity, to discover and formulate our own opinions, to develop our ability to reflect and to make our own conscious choices; and it acknowledges and validates the rights of others to do the same.

When we engage with life through empathy, the quality of respect enables difference to be welcomed with interest, rather than received as a threat and as something to be defended against, and this creates possibility for learning and for growth. Doorways are open, and there is a mutual flow of both giving and receiving.

We often hear the term give and take in relationships. When I think about a healthy exchange, within a relationship, I prefer to think about giving and receiving.

Giving and receiving are different to giving and taking.

Taking and Receiving are not the same.

When we take, whoever or whatever we take from, may or may not have chosen to give to us, choice may be absent. However, when we receive, choice and healthy respect are inherently part of the exchange. Indeed, when we take, we deprive someone the opportunity of giving.

True empathy cannot exist without respect. Respect creates a purity in our relational exchange. Respect ensures that the exchange is non-judgemental, and non-directive whilst still maintaining a space of potential negotiation.

Yes and No are active participants in any form of negotiation and when they walk hand in hand with respect, they become key ingredients in our ability to embrace conscious and mindful choice.

Yes and No are a dynamic relationship, they are two sides of the same coin, and yet many people struggle with this Yes/No partnership, particularly when it comes to saying No.

Sometimes, people are afraid that saying No will make them an ungiving or an uncaring person. Actually this is far from the truth.

When we say No to something that is inappropriate or unhealthy, by acknowledging that something isn't okay, this recognition actually creates an opportunity for change. So, even if we find ourselves facing a

7 Steps to Spiritual Empathy, a Practical Guide

challenging situation, in truth, saying a healthy No opens doorways of possibility.

When we say No in any unhealthy situation we are saying Yes to life.

In any exchange, and in any negotiation, regardless of the actual circumstance there is an underlying emotional currency involved, an underlying emotional exchange taking place, and both Yes and No have the potential to carry with them both a positive or a negative charge.

When someone gives us something by choice, born of free will, with love, desire and joy, as well as the actual something, the exchange will also carry the emotional gifts of love, desire and joy. The exchange will bring the feel good factor with it. However, when something is given through obligation, guilt or fear the exchange will feel very different. On the surface the situation may appear to be identical, however, the underlying emotional exchange is made of some very challenging emotions. There is no feel good factor here and the exchange is carrying a very different meaning.

True respect comes without any obligation, there is no agenda and no ulterior motive, simply a desire to be open to both giving and receiving. There is a mutuality in the field between us, a mutuality in the exchange between us, and both yes and no remain the property of both parties.

Our ability to say both Yes and No from a position of self-responsibility defines our capacity to own our own choices, it defines our ability to do as we say and to walk our talk, and indeed, when needed, it demonstrates our ability to draw the line and to stand our ground, to hold onto and stand firm in the wisdom of our experience.

When Yes and No are delivered with integrity, respect will be inherent in the exchange, and this forms an integral part of our capacity to engage fully in self-care, as well as in the care of those around us.

When we offer and treat ourselves with respect, we are developing self-respect. Self-respect fuels self-esteem.

When our self-esteem and our inner sense of self value is healthy, we recognise our own needs and our own healthy limits and our own

46

humanness. We recognise our autonomy and we take responsibility for negotiating our choices.

When we offer and treat others with respect we recognize their needs, their opinions, and their differences. When we treat someone with respect we recognise their autonomy and therefore the responsibility that they have for their own actions.

I have a very dear friend who often uses the term "Tread Lightly through Life". When he uses these words he is referring to a gentle approach to life, where he strives to live respectfully, not to "tread on the toes" of others. He is however, no push over, and his clarity of boundaries would serve as a role model for us all. By treading lightly, he is striving to live from a position in which respect is woven into the very fabric of his considered choices and actions.

Living respectfully means living honourably. Even when faced with inappropriate action on the part of others, in living respectfully, we demonstrate by example.

When we live with honour we reinforce our own self-value and therefore our self-esteem. Honour and self-respect enable us to remain steady and resilient, whilst also holding desire for a potential resolution. Our empathic ability to receive, with interest, enquiry and a desire to look more deeply with understanding and with compassion will support and define both our own autonomy as well as the autonomy of others.

Our empathic ability to receive, with interest, enquiry and a desire to look more deeply with understanding and with compassion will enable us to bring to our awareness all that we receive with honest appreciation and gratitude, and with this in mind we can consciously consider our choices and intentions with awareness of the wider implications of our actions.

Our intentions and our actions are the birthplace of manifestation. If we wish to live in a world that holds respect dear, then we will need to live respectfully.

We have a choice.

We can tread lightly and travel mindfully, and in recognizing all that we receive, we can consciously consider all that we may in turn give back.

7 Steps to Spiritual Empathy, a Practical Guide

My Thought for the Day

Living Respectfully is the Foundation of my Well-being.

My Invitation

Today I wish to invite you to deepen your awareness of what it means to "Tread Lightly" in your life. Where does respect sit in your interactions with yourself, with others and in your life in general?

My Thoughts and Suggestions

Take some time to bring your attention to your interactions and with the kinds of exchanges that have taken place during your day.

Have you felt respected and do you feel you have offered and shown respect to others?

Have your exchanges been mutually respectful?

Are there any situations in your life where you find yourself saying Yes, when you would have preferred to say No?

On our journey together we have been learning to notice, to listen and to observe our emotions, without judgement or criticism. As you reflect, notice any underlying emotions that were part of the exchange, in both yourself as well as the other party and be mindful to consider these without judgement or blame.

Respect isn't something that we say, it is something that we do.

We cannot be in charge of the actions of others. We are however, in charge of our own choices.

As you consider your own actions and interactions throughout the day, notice and ask yourself these questions;

- Were my actions and interactions **Considered**?

- Are the consequences of my actions and interactions **Considerate**?
- **Considerate** of my own well-being?
- **Considerate** of the well-being of others?
- And **Considerate** of the well-being of the wider environment around me?

As we develop our ability to notice and as we deepen our awareness of the ways in which we ourselves are living and of the consequences and outcomes of our own actions, we can begin to consider how we ourselves might approach things differently. In doing so we take conscious charge of our ability to journey through life respectfully.

Our choices, our intentions and our actions are active in creating the kind of world that we wish to live in, and active in co-creating the kind of world that we wish to leave behind for future generations.

We have a choice.

"We will be known forever from the tracks we leave behind"

Lakota proverb.

Chapter 5

The Fifth Principle of Empathy

"Responsiveness"

"Life isn't about finding yourself. Life is about creating yourself."

George Bernard Shaw.

Born 1856, Playwright.

Whether we offer empathy to others, or to ourselves, when our mind and our emotions meet and collaborate, this sharing of information and experience, creates opportunity for conscious choice, and therefore opportunity for change.

For most of us empathy has very peaceful associations and so we don't necessarily tend to associate it with action, but in truth, pure empathy holds a very active position. Even when we simply pause to listen, we are still taking a considered action.

Listening is often thought of as a passive occupation, but in truth empathic listening, whilst still and grounded in the present, is actually a very active state of being. Empathic listening involves being able to receive, and to reflect, with respectful consideration, before then deciding how to respond. Even if our decision is to choose to do nothing as yet, it is still a considered and thought through response.

So responsiveness implies taking some kind of an action, an action that emerges from the seeds of consideration. A responsive action involves being aware and mindful of both ourselves and of others, mindful of the immediacy of our world as well as mindful of our dynamic connection and resonance within a larger universe ; it involves an awareness of conscious choice, a **"Re-sponse"** born of our ability to be present and to receive our real, here and now emotional experience, combined with reflective thought; rather than a **"Re-action"** where experience arrives and triggers automated and un-thought through behaviour or words.

We have spoken about the need to create space within; a space free of emotionally held tension and stress; a space free of unwelcoming, judgemental or critically held perceptions of our mind.

If the space within is cluttered and we are carrying the burden of unresolved emotional problems within us, then as long as unresolved tension and history remains ignored and unheard, it will colour our perceptions and continue to influence our responses, often unconsciously.

When faced with an emotionally challenging situation, we are far more likely to **"Re-act"** rather than **"Re-spond"**. Our history will be directing us and this will stand in the way of us being present to the immediacy of our experience of life, right here and right now.

Our perceptions will be coloured by the emotional content that we have accumulated. There will be a lack of space, and a lack of availability, to listen to and to process our real, here and now experience, with reflection and mindful consideration.

When we live through true empathy, we can welcome not only our here and now emotional experience, with reflective compassionate thinking; we can also choose to welcome any emotionally laden history that we have accumulated, and through respectful, considered, reflective thought, decide how we might respond, and decide on the actions that we need to take. We can become actively engaged in our choices.

I am sure we've all heard the saying, "hindsight is a wonderful thing" and from an emotional point of view, this is absolutely true.

When we experience something that is difficult or challenging, painful or hurtful, if we are able to actively listen to this information, rather than reacting in ways that are unconscious or that we have learned at an earlier stage in our lives, we can explore and consider other options and alternative courses of action.

We can learn from our experiences and we can grow from our experiences. We can build on our experiences and naturally integrate them into our bank of growth and knowledge.

And whilst we may draw on the past, we don't have to live through the past.

There is a difference.

Learning to listen and be responsive to ourselves will open doorways of opportunity that are literally life changing. Hindsight truly is a wonderful thing.

All of us will at some time or another feel the need to "off-load" when something is bothering us. We need to "let off steam". And this is generally an emotional outpouring, we are venting our feelings.

When we "vent", we are pouring emotional content into the energetic field around us, often with little comprehension or understanding of the impact it will have on both ourselves as well as others and in the wider field around us.

However, if we can pause and listen to what is really driving our discontent; if we can see beyond the surface **re-action** and listen to that which sits below the surface, we can begin to hear what is really driving us and in doing so we can make considered, mindful, decisions about what we might wish to do and what actions we may need to take.

When we take time to listen to others with empathy we afford them the same opportunity.

When we live through empathy, we become actively in charge of the choices that are available to us. The intelligence of our heart, and the intelligence of our mind, walk hand-in-hand, in a united relationship, centred in compassion, care and respect. Emotionally laden experiences,

7 Steps to Spiritual Empathy, a Practical Guide

past as well as present, can arrive, be welcomed and considered, and this active process of deepening awareness creates opportunity for conscious choice with active conscious responses.

True empathy holds space for creative thought and responsive action.

True Empathy fuels the development of our self-awareness, and the development of our awareness of others.

True Empathy heightens our appreciation of all that we receive and of all that we can give.

True empathy is a foundation stone in our ability to offer care to ourselves, others and the world at large.

True empathy creates awareness of consequence and therefore opportunity for self-responsible, co-creative living that is actively engaged in the process of natural evolutionary growth.

Whether we offer empathy to others or to ourselves, the collaboration of our mind and our emotions create availability to be fully present and fully available to life itself. When we live through empathy we actively choose to become a responsive partner within the dance of our own life.

My Thought for Today

I Choose to Live Through Responsive Choice.

My Invitation

Today I wish to invite you to develop your skills in actively listening and in doing so to take a consciously chosen, responsive and considered action.

My Thoughts and Suggestions

We often think about choice in relation to the big decisions in our lives, however in reality, each and every day we make countless choices, many of which we do automatically, without necessarily listening to what might be motivating us to make that choice.

We also, each and every day make decisions about choosing **NOT** to do something. It is so easy to be critical of things that we see around us. In truth, if we bear witness to a problem or a situation that isn't ok, this actually presents us with an opportunity. By noticing and becoming aware, we have an opportunity to make a conscious and responsive choice about the part that we ourselves may be able to play in changing that situation.

Notice and become aware of the number of choices you make every day, choices made in which you are actively **"doing"**, and also choices made in which you are actively choosing **"NOT"** to do something.

Take a particular situation and give yourself time and space to listen.

- **Listen** with your ears. What information are you hearing? Factual information, words, language, tone of voice? **Listen?**
- **Listen** with your eyes. What are you seeing, what can you hear with your eyes? What actions are taken? Can you see consequences and outcomes of previous actions? Is there a

repetition of a pattern or similar behaviour? What emotions are visually present? What body language do you see? Can you see a re-action rather than a re-sponse? **Listen?**

- **Listen** with your body. What is your "gut feeling" telling you? Where in your body are you experiencing this situation? We experience emotions in our physical body, (2) in fact there are many sayings that give us clues about the way our body carries emotional experience. We "shoulder" responsibility. It got "under my skin". I had a "lump in my throat". What emotions are present and where do they sit within you? **Listen?**

- **Listen** through your heart. What do you feel in your heart? What are the emotions and feelings that are channelling through your heart? What is your heart telling you? **Listen?**

- **Listen** with your mind. What do your thoughts tell you? We all have an inner dialogue. Is your mind critical of the situation? Critical of either yourself or others, or are your thoughts positive, encouraging and supportive? Do your thoughts anticipate the best or the worst outcome? What are your thoughts telling you to believe? What kinds of beliefs and values are your thoughts generating and reinforcing? **Listen?**

Listening gives us good information and this information is there to give us assistance and to inform active and conscious decision making, choices that spring from conscious self-awareness. Awareness of ourselves, awareness of others, and indeed awareness of the bigger picture, awareness of our environment and world around us.

Taking this empathic and mindful listening into account I wish to invite you, at least once today, to make a decision that is truly and actively responsive. Whether **doing** or choosing **NOT** to do, to the very best of your ability make a responsive choice followed through with a responsive action. A responsive action born of reflective listening with respectful care and consideration, an action born of empathy.

"Awareness without action is worthless."

Phil McGraw

Born 1956. Psychologist.

---

2 For further reading in this area I would suggest "The Body Keeps the Score". Bessel Van Der Kolk, MD.

Chapter 6

The Sixth Principle of Empathy

"Resolution"

"Resolve, and thou art free."

Henry Wadsworth Longfellow.

Born 1807. Poet.

As we continue our journey with empathy, we can begin to understand that by its very nature, empathy embodies and creates the possibility of change and growth.

Empathy creates an internal space that offers us a holding ground for experience, a space where our heart and our mind can meet and sit in counsel. But this space is not a holding ground of permanence. It is a space of movement, transition and transformation.

Whilst reflective, being empathic is not about holding on to stuff. Being empathic is being fully present, fully open and fully available to receive, to reflect, and to respectfully respond. And in responding appropriately, we transform the content of experience in a way that enables us to grow through experience, and from experience.

Being empathic creates opportunity for transformation and change and therefore, by its very nature, it creates opportunity for potential resolution.

Our experiences are the substance of our growth. Our experiences make up the building blocks of our journey throughout our lives and fuel our ability to form our opinions and to develop meaning in life.

When we learn from our experiences and we grow from our experiences, we are building on experience. We are integrating experience into our bank of knowledge, and it is from this transformational process that we are able to draw on the past in ways that inform us on our journey.

Drawing on the past is not the same as living through the past. There is a difference.

If we find ourselves still living through some element of our past, or if we find ourselves continually re-experiencing our current life through the lens of our history in ways that no longer serve us, then we will need to be able to process and re-file this experience, so that it can become **"Re-membered"**, rather than **"Re-lived"**. **"Re-membered"** rather than **"Re-experienced"**.

Empathy gifts us with this opportunity.

Living through empathy affords us the choice to become actively responsive, not only to our here and now experience, but also to any historical difficulties that may still be presenting themselves in our current time. Living through empathy affords us the opportunity to process any emotionally laden history, that we may still be carrying.

When we receive, we develop our ability to listen without judgement.

When we reflect, we develop our capacity to notice and to consider.

When we live with respect, we develop our capacity to forgive, both ourselves as well as others.

When we are responsive, we develop our capacity to heal and to repair.

All of these qualities firm up and give definition to the structures that surround the space within, so that the very substance of that internal space can become a melting pot of ingredients that combined and mixed together, create a space of evolutionary transformation. A space of integration and resolution, where experience is made sense of in a way that enables us to file it away as memory. Memory which feeds and fuels our continuing journey through life.

Even if we are unable to identify the exact origins of something, when we notice that the storyline we are currently living is not as we would wish it to be. By noticing what is taking place in our here and now time, and by identifying any subsequent patterns of behaviour, we can recognise any re-actions that don't really belong in our present time, and that are no longer serving us.

It is entirely possible to reach a resolution of a past experience through the resolution of something that is taking place in our present time, a situation in our here and now, that is resonating with a past scenario.

Cutting edge research in epigenetics (3) has shown us that traumatic experience leaves a kind of memory in our physical body, a kind of molecular scar that affects and alters our DNA, and that this memory can be passed down genetically to future generations. When this memory re-surfaces it can be re-experienced as an emotional memory, an emotional state of experience, or indeed an emotional state of re-experience that contains fear and trauma; a memory of a residual emotional experience of fear and trauma that is held within our physical body. There may be no consciously known understanding of the origins of this experience, and yet it lives within us. An **"unthought known"** (4) sitting within our personal field of energy, influencing and affecting our lives, right here and right now.

So if we consider that we carry many different kinds of memories from the past; memories that are both known, as well as some that are unknown; memories that have taken place within our own lifetime, as well as a memory or residue of past happenings that have taken place either in our own very early life or indeed potentially in generations before us, and as we have already acknowledged, science has shown us that the residue of past experiences can be inherited and passed down to us at a cellular level; if a situation arrives in our current time, and we find ourselves following a repeating pattern, however challenging this may be, it actually presents us with an opportunity. It presents us with an opportunity to reach some kind of resolution within the here and now.

Sometimes when circumstances have remained unresolved we can find ourselves drawn back to certain people or even drawn to similar types of situations or similar types of people again and again. This is completely natural, we are searching for a conclusion and instinctively want something to change, we are searching for a satisfactory outcome and some kind of closure.

When history repeats itself, or rather as the residue of history resurfaces and arrives again through a current experience, listening and responding through empathy will enable whatever is taking place in the here and now to be received with interest, inquiry and discovery, creating an opportunity to process and to work through any underlying issues within the context of a current situation.

It is often through adversity that we grow.

It is often through adversity that we discover meaning.

Whether we are relating to ourselves or to others, empathy enables us to appreciate the growth and the learning that we have gained from any situation. When we seek a resolution we are looking to transform the nature of the way that we both think and feel about a situation. Empathy enables us to appreciate the way in which our history has contributed to who we have become. Empathy enables us to understand how our history has contributed in making us the person that we are today.

History doesn't have to continue to repeat itself.

When we develop our capacity to listen and to be responsive to what is actually taking place in the immediacy of our lives right now, history can find its rightful place in the past and become integrated into our memory bank of experience.

Empathy offers us this gift. Empathy gives us this choice.

Sometimes our inability to recognise the choices that are available to us, or perhaps our inability to want to recognise the choices that are available to us, perhaps because they are not those that we would wish to have, can cause us to reject opportunity or back down from the possibility of change.

Every day we are presented with a multitude of choices, doorways of opportunity that are available in front of us, available to be opened and walked through. If we are unable to live in a manner that is present to our immediate experience and we cannot listen to our immediate experience, then we may not even see these doorways, let alone find the courage to walk through them.

When we live through empathy we become a space for the integration and the resolution of past experience. The presence of our emotional voice in conversation with our extraordinary mind, creates the possibility for transformation and creative change and therefore for resolution and potential closure of the past.

What does closure really mean?

When we talk about **"reaching closure"** we are not talking about a definitive end. It doesn't mean that history will vanish and that we will cease to remember. Reaching closure is a marking of time, a placing of something into its rightful place in our history.

When we integrate past experience in ways that create learning, growth and meaning, we can separate our past from our present. Reaching closure is a process. When we recognise history and we notice and bring something to our attention, and through compassionate understanding we honour the growth that has come from this, we will no longer need to continue re-enacting unresolved struggles by regenerating them again and again.

When honour, appreciation and gratitude become the defining qualities of the space within, even through adversity, our experience becomes one of growth and therefore of potential transformation.

We can choose to step out of habitual patterns of re-action. We can re-file experience, and lay to rest the re-playing of history, and in doing so we create the opportunity for an entirely different life, an entirely different way of living.

7 Steps to Spiritual Empathy, a Practical Guide

When we receive ourselves, in a state of empathy, regardless of our past, in generating change right here and right now, we can actively choose to redefine ourselves, and in doing so we take responsibility for redefining our future.

When we sit in a place of compassionate interest and enquiry with ourselves, open to receive and to learn then we will be able to offer the same to others.

My Thought for Today

My History Has Made Me Who I am Today.

My Invitation

Sometimes the most challenging and difficult periods in our lives create a kind of doorway to a greater level of awareness, a place in time when we shift to a greater level of consciousness.

Today I wish to invite you to identify a past experience that has contributed to your core values. The core values that you hold dear and that give your life meaning and form the substance of what it means to be you.

My Thoughts and Suggestions

It is often through adversity that we learn our biggest lessons in life.

It is often through adversity that we discover meaning.

I would like to invite you to write a list of your most important core values. The values that make up the substance of who you are, the substance of what it means to you to be human. The kinds of qualities that matter to you and the qualities through which you wish and aspire to live.

For example, kindness, care, honesty, fairness, a sense of justice, courage, compassion, a desire to do something differently.

Then take some time to cast your mind back to a difficult or challenging experience in your life and ask yourself the following questions;

- How did this experience contribute to the development of my core values?
- What did I learn from this experience that has fuelled my growth and my understanding?
- Did this experience help to consolidate my core values?

- What kinds of life skills have I developed because of this experience?
- How has this experience contributed to who I am today?

Our core values may not be visible to the world at large but like a tree, regardless of the strength of the wind, it is the depth of the roots, unseen and below the surface, that keep it grounded. It is the depth of the roots and strength of the core that grows from them, that enables a tree to stand firm whilst bending and dancing with the wind.

When we have an appreciation of what we have learned, even through adversity, we gain meaning from experience. Our past becomes the roots of who have become, integrated within us in ways that strengthens our resilience and our durability. History can be laid to rest and as we navigate transition to a new and a better place and we find resolution, our past becomes the very the core of our inner strength.

"Do not let the future be held hostage by the past."

Neal A. Maxwell

Born 1926. Apostle, Author, Administrator, and Educator.

3 Further suggested reading "Super Genes". Rudolph E Tanzi and Deepak Chopra. 4 "The Shadow of the Object, Psychoanalysis of the Unthought Known". Christopher Bollas

Chapter 7

The Seventh Principle of Empathy

"Relationship"

"Humankind has not woven the web of life. We are but one thread within it. Whatever we do to the web, we do to ourselves. All things are bound together. All things connect."

Chief Seattle.

Born 1780. Chief of the Suquamish Tribe.

A s we come to the end our journey we meet the seventh and the most fundamental principle of empathy. **Relationship.**

Relationship, is at the very core of what it is to be human. **Relationship,** and indeed **Relating,** is at the very core of what it is to be alive. We are in a continual state of relating and relatedness all of the time.

Whether we are talking about being in relationship with ourselves, or in relationship with others. Whether we are talking about the relationship between mind, body and spirit, whether we are talking about being in relationship with nature or in relationship with a spiritual experience of life, and in relationship with a greater universal intelligence, being alive is about being **"in relationship"**. And the greater our awareness of this, the greater our ability to live through conscious choice.

Throughout this book I have placed a great deal of emphasis on our relationship with ourselves. I do so with good intent. In order to offer empathy to others, indeed to live in a manner that allows us to tread lightly through life and to live life with true respect and consideration, we will need to develop our ability to be fully relational and to do this we will need to know and understand ourselves. To be able to live through conscious choice, we will need to become aware of ourselves, and there is no better way to relate and to understand ourselves than to receive ourselves through empathy.

Empathy is the very fabric of relatedness.

True empathy, is relational multitasking at its best. Just as our bodies are designed to multitask; they do it all of the time, without any prompting at all from our mind; our lungs are breathing, our heart is beating, and every cell in our body is continually reproducing and functioning in exactly the way that it is designed to. This is the natural way of living, this is the natural way of being, our body is an active participant in life.

So too, when we live through empathy, our mind and our emotions collaborate and multitask at their best. We are receiving, we are reflecting, we are respectfully responsive, and we take considered action. This is the natural way of living; this is the natural way of being. We are an active participant in life.

Empathy enables us to be fully present to our real here and now experience, and through the immediacy of this experience empathy grants us the opportunity for a connection that can heal across time. Within our present experience empathy enables us to listen to our history whilst actively considering our future. Regardless of what has taken place in our past, empathy enables our mind and our emotions to join forces and become active in our transformation.

When we live through empathy we live through our real experience with enquiry, curiosity and discovery, and in becoming present to our here and now experience we become a space for resolution and integration.

Integration is the birthplace of integrity. To integrate and to become whole we need to be living through relationship, with an internal space of availability to process the experiences that life is giving us.

Integration is not an end goal, it's a journey, and empathy enables us to be present and fully available to participate in that journey.

To live well and to lead a healthy adult life, we will need to embrace self-responsibility and healthy self-care, balanced with an awareness of the needs of others. We will need to become mindful of the consequences of our actions, both in the immediacy of our own lives as well as in a wider context.

Some people are very good at looking after others but not themselves, whilst others live life from a more self-orientated position. Whenever there is an inconsistency in our capacity to relate, a discrepancy between the way in which we treat ourselves and the way in which we treat others, regardless of whether our actions are either **"self-less"** or **"self-ish"**, we are creating an in-balance and this will have a resonance in the world.

We are all but one part of the web, uniquely autonomous and yet intrinsically connected, separate and yet inseparable.

Empathy is the very fabric of connectedness.

A life without empathy is a life without connection. A life being lived that is, to a very great extent, disengaged from life itself. It is a life of survival rather than a life of aliveness. A life of coping and getting by rather than a life of thriving and flourishing. A way of existing where life is defended against, rather than embraced.

When we embrace self-responsibility through the core principals of empathy, with pride in the growth of our own autonomy, we are free to be fully relational, free to fully experience ourselves as part of a greater unity, whilst being present to our here and now human experience. With reflection and consideration, we are available to engage in mindful conversation, not only with ourselves and with others, but with all that surrounds and supports us.

69

Autonomy doesn't mean separateness from the world. It means relatedness with the world.

I believe that it is unhelpful to separate spirituality from daily life or regard it as a separate entity. I am not suggesting for one moment that we should not consciously make time for specific spiritual practise, such as prayer or meditation, but rather that we embrace all of life from a place of spiritual consideration, including of course, space and time to honour our individual beliefs and practises.

To live a spiritual existence is a way of life. To live a spiritual existence is to tread lightly. Empathy gifts us with this possibility.

Living through empathy is a way of living and a way of being that regardless of our individual religious beliefs, supports us in experiencing each and every moment from a place of deep and profound connectedness and relatedness with all aspects of life itself.

This deep and profound connectedness within ourselves will in turn be reflected in our relatedness and our connection with our external world. True empathy supports us in becoming fully awake and fully present.

Being fully present involves intimacy, and to truly thrive and to engage with life at its fullest involves an intimacy with all aspects of living. Empathy brings about a deeply intimate connection with life, a deeply spiritual experience of what it means to be alive. When we live through empathy, we are intimately and deeply involved in relationship with life itself.

When we live through empathy we retain our ability to experience life with the openness and awe of a child, walking hand in hand with an adult whose perspective stems from the wisdom of a life being lived.

Pure empathy is a divine state of being, a divine state of relatedness, fluid and yet strong and resilient; a state of both giving and receiving with conscious awareness, a conscious exchange that embraces an openness and an availability that is in turn contained and held within the boundaries of mindful discernment.

Empathy is both boundary and space, definition and infiniteness. Empathy enables us to sit in relationship with the seen as well as the unseen, it bridges relational boundaries enabling us to create a meeting place between not only our mind and our emotions, but a meeting place between our past and present and indeed our future. A meeting place between our human experience and a spiritual pathway of living, a pathway of connectedness, a pathway of being.

Empathy supports us in maintaining a free flow of energy, through empathy we create a space of possibility in which we can actively embrace conscious intention. Living through empathy IS living through relationship. We are present and in relationship with right now and what we do right now will determine who we are becoming.

When we embrace conscious intention we are actively co-creating our future. We are literally dreaming with our eyes wide open.

When we embrace conscious intention through the principles of empathy, rather than dreaming of "having more", we dream of "being more".

My Thought for Today

I Dream with my Eyes Wide Open.

My Invitation

Today I wish to invite you to dream through the eyes of empathy.

My Thoughts and Suggestions

Firstly, I wish to invite you for one moment to consider how a world might look in which all of humanity engaged with life through the principles of spiritual empathy. A world of mutual giving and receiving, interwoven with reflective considered thoughts and actions born of respect and integrity.

This may seem a somewhat idealistic picture of the world, however if we cannot dream then we will never take the steps needed for the vision to become real.

When a writer begins a story or an artist a painting, they will have an idea of what they are aiming for, they will have a vision or a dream of what they aspire to achieve. Without the dream they wouldn't be motivated to begin and the process of creative change would never get started.

Let us now bring our dreaming into the space of our immediate world.

I wish to invite you to bring to mind something that you would like to be different.

Now let us dream about this situation through the principles of spiritual empathy.

Firstly, let's create a space within, where noticing is the primary desire, and let us view the situation from the perspective of ourselves as the source of potential change.

Let us now receive the situation.

Let us invite both our mind and our emotions to the stage. Let us notice the way that we feel about this situation. How are our emotions informing us? What do we need to hear?

And now let us notice our thoughts. As we receive and pay attention to our full experience of the situation let us make space for considered reflection. As we play with possibilities in our mind, do any new insights arrive?

As we consider the situation from all perspectives, let us then bring the questions back to ourselves.

Where do we sit in relationship with this situation and what would be the most respectful way forwards?

How might we consider responding and what, if anything, can we do towards initiating change? The most respectful way forwards may involve taking immediate action. However, it might also involve an in-action, taking more time to look in-wards to reflect and consider.

Can a resolution be sought and what would constitute a valuable outcome?

As we allow ourselves to dream in mindful contemplation, welcoming both our heart, as well as our mind, answers and ways forwards will inevitably arrive as they should.

When we listen with everything that we are, the answers that we dream will have a quality of meaning that resonates with our soul. Indeed, when our decision making process becomes one of relational spirituality our subsequent actions become aligned and balanced with a greater knowing, and a reflection of a greater purpose.

Living through the principles of spiritual empathy enables us to discover what it means to be a true human **"being"**.

"Don't look for your dreams to come true; look to become true to your dreams."

Reverend Michael Beckwith

Born 1956. Author, American New Thought minister, Founder of the Agape International Spiritual Center.

Conclusion.

"What Can We Learn from a Blade of Grass?"

"The pattern of life is not woven ahead of time, like cloth to be worn later as a tunic.

Rather life is woven at the very instant you live it."

Brian Bates.

Born 1944. Author of "The Way of Wyrd".

Many years ago I started reading a book about quantum physics. Now whilst I didn't understand the mathematics, I immediately related to and understood the nature of what I was reading, I understood it in terms of an exchange of energy. And not only did I understand it as a concept, I understood it in terms of my therapeutic work.

I knew that when I sit, engaged "in relationship" with another, that an energetic exchange takes place between us, and that the nature of this exchange is not simply about thought. It is also about emotion.

The energetic content between us is shaped and coloured by the combination of thought and emotion, and when our purpose and core intention is one of a mutual desire for change, the extraordinary union of mind and emotion creates a transformational space of healing with opportunity for a person to discover within themselves an inherent way of relating that embraces growth and learning as a natural evolutionary way of living.

For most of us our biggest hurts in life stem from some kind of relational difficulty. It is predominantly through relationship, or indeed the absence of relationship, that we feel most damaged. It is also through relationship that we can repair.

So what can we learn from a blade of grass?

Many people fear change, even though they desperately desire it. In truth, regardless of whether we embrace or resist, life itself is an ongoing journey of change. We are in a continual state of growth and therefore in a continual state of change.

Grass is a resilient plant, extraordinary in its ordinariness. In tune with the seasons it grows with renowned consistency. Its capacity to grow is unstoppable and its connectedness to evolutionary growth inherent.

Writer Ilya Ehrenburg puts it so well. "You could cover the whole earth with asphalt, but sooner or later green grass would break through."

I love the use of the words "break through".

Without striving and without force grass simply adapts to whatever conditions it is faced with and in tune with life itself, it simply keeps on growing, becoming everything that it was designed to be.

We too are growing, and at times will inevitably be faced with challenging situations, however, unlike a blade of grass, as adult human beings we have the extraordinary opportunity to take ownership of our learning. We have the unique opportunity to embrace our own autonomy and to develop our awareness and our self-responsibility and therefore ownership of our choices and our direction.

Self-responsibility does not mean going it alone.

However, there is a difference between receiving support in the making our own decisions, as opposed to desiring others to make decisions for us. As adults, when we look to others to meet our needs or hold them responsible for the shape of our world, we are effectively giving them responsibility for our well-being and in doing so we place ourselves in a passive position.

When we step away from self-responsibility we relinquish the opportunity to become aware of any part that we ourselves may have played in the scenario, and in doing so we give away our personal power. We give away our entitlement and our opportunity to have a conscious say in finding a co-creative resolution and we relinquish our opportunity to be actively engaged in navigating our way forwards.

Dare to dream, and dare to see yourself as the source of any potential change.

There will always be times in our lives when we are faced with difficult and challenging situations and as adults what we make of those experiences and what we do in response to them will to a very great extent determine whether a challenging experience becomes one of growth and learning or one that compounds feelings of helplessness and further difficulty; a situation of breakdown or an opportunity for break through.

Stepping into a place of relational spirituality and embracing life through the principals of empathy is a journey, and one that requires gentle nurturing with forgiveness of both ourselves as well as others, with a celebration of the learning curve to be found in both our mistakes and our disappointments as well as our celebrations.

Unresolved emotional history has a habit of reappearing in our current time. When we are fully present to our real here and now experience, our capacity to listen with all that we are, creates opportunity for emotional healing and opportunity to become all that we can be.

Regardless of what has taken place in either our own past or the residue of a past that we may have inherited, empathy enables us to experience ourselves with enquiry, curiosity and discovery and in becoming present to our here and now experience we create opportunity for potential change.

Empathy is the gift that brings us this possibility.

As we integrate the principals of spiritual empathy into our daily lives we can listen to any history that is re-appearing in the current time, whilst consciously considering our future.

As we integrate the principals of spiritual empathy into our daily lives we learn to ask ourselves questions and to value inquiry. We learn to look more deeply, allowing time for a responsive direction to evolve and to emerge and we develop the relational skills that enable us to seek counsel and support whilst retaining our capacity for free will and choice.

We are writing our story and painting our picture right here and right now. We are spinning the web whilst living within it. When we choose to meet with life through the principles of spiritual empathy we consciously presence ourselves within this process. We are autonomous and yet connected, independent and yet inter-dependent.

Embracing a life of relational spirituality doesn't mean that we will be happy all of the time. It is our lessons learned through both joy as well as adversity that bring us a truly integrated appreciation and value of all that we have and all that we are, and through our very being, all that we are creating and becoming moment by moment.

"Every great dream begins with a dreamer. Always remember, you have within you the strength, the patience, and the passion to reach for the stars to change the world."

Harriet Tubman

Born 1820. Anti-slavery Activist, Humanitarian.

About the Author and about this Series of Books.

"If Our Eyes are the Windows of Our Soul, then Our Emotions are the Voice of Our Soul."

Jenny Florence.

Born 1961, Therapist, Writer, Mother.

I have worked as an accredited counsellor and therapist for many many years now, listening to people of all ages, men, women, couples and individuals, each and every one a unique and individual human being on their own unique and individual journey and I have come to the conclusion that the area of our lives where the majority of us seem to struggle most is intrinsically connected to our emotions, and I myself am no exception to the rule.

Our growing up, our families, our relationships, life events and the everyday happenings of life leave their mark, and this mark is an emotional one.

In my own life I have had some pretty challenging experiences including childhood depression and a several abusive friendships and relationships in my adult life. Those were very challenging times and whilst I clearly didn't enjoy the way that I was feeling, **I can say without exception that**

79

every emotion that I felt was a natural response to a situation in my life that wasn't ok. These challenging emotions were giving me "good information" and I needed to listen to them.

And not only did I need to listen to them in relation to the immediate circumstances I was in, but I also needed to travel inwards more deeply to recognize when I was bringing emotional history forwards into my current life.

We cannot change our past but it has certainly been my own experience that we can change our relationship to our past, and in doing so we create change within our present, which in turn changes the shape of our future.

If we work on the premise that in our adult lives we ourselves "ARE" the source of potential change, it becomes clear that we will need to be able listen to ourselves without fear and without judgement.

Our emotions are a powerful, human commodity.

They can be our strongest and most supportive ally in life, or they can disable us, leaving us feeling blocked or at worst, out of control and in pieces.

In my experience it is never the emotion itself that's the problem, it's our relationship to it and our ability to listen to this information and choose what we do with it that will make the difference between a challenging experience being a break through, rather than a break down, a challenge or a crisis.

I know that my deepening ability to listen to my emotions and to consider every emotional state that I feel as **"valuable information"** has created a way of living that in itself has been life changing.

This is the first in a series of books about the intelligence of our emotions, each written to support and enable deepening layers of relational growth and understanding.

The format of the book is deliberate. I hope that its bite sized chapters will make it accessible, easy to read and above all translatable into a kind of emotional tool kit that can pragmatically help to integrate emotional awareness into daily living in ways that will enhance all aspects of who we are and who we wish to become.

Thank you.

7 Steps to Spiritual Empathy, a Practical Guide

Work with Jenny

Jenny is both a Writer and Speaker. She is also the Author and Creator of the A-Z of Emotional Health on-line Audio Library.

To contact Jenny or for more information and to register to receive updates about her work including free Audios and Meditations please go to www.jennyflorencehealth.com

To access her on-line Audio Library go to www.a-z-of-emotionalhealth.com

To Download the Worksheets that accompany this book and the Free Meditation "The Transformational Power of Emotion" go to www.spiritualempathy.com/meditation/

References.

Mackay, Harvey. (n.d.). BrainyQuote.com. Retrieved June 1, 2016, from BrainyQuote.com Web site:
http://www.brainyquote.com/quotes/quotes/h/harveymack528736.html

Sarandon, Susan (n.d.). BrainyQuote.com. Retrieved June 1, 2016, from BrainyQuote.com Web site:
http://www.brainyquote.com/quotes/quotes/s/susansaran371309.html

Redfield, James. The Celestine Prophecy. New York: Warner Books, 1996

Chopra, Deepak. (n.d.). BrainyQuote.com. Retrieved April 21, 2016, from BrainyQuote.com Web site:
http://www.brainyquote.com/quotes/quotes/d/deepakchop599950.html

Teilhard de Chardin, Pierre. (n.d.). BrainyQuote.com. Retrieved February 28, 2016, from BrainyQuote.com Web site:
http://www.brainyquote.com/quotes/quotes/p/pierreteil160888.html

Frankl, Viktor. Man's Search For Meaning. Beacon Press; 1 edition (June 1, 2006)

Tse, Lao. Tao Te Ching. London: Wildwood House Ltd. Translation by Gia-Fu Feng and Jane English, 1972

Blum, Ralph. http://effortlesspeace.com/stillness-quotes/

Rumi, Mewlana Jalaluddin. The Guest House. The Essential Rumi. Penguin Classics; New Ed edition (24 Jun. 2004)

Goleman, Daniel. Emotional Intelligence. Bloomsbury Publishing PLC; New edition 1996

Zukav, Gary. (n.d.). BrainyQuote.com. Retrieved April 6, 2016, from BrainyQuote.com Web site:
http://www.brainyquote.com/quotes/quotes/g/garyzukav637594.html

Proust, Marcel. (n.d.). BrainyQuote.com. Retrieved April 6, 2016, from BrainyQuote.com Web site: http://www.brainyquote.com/quotes/quotes/m/marcelprou107111.html

Hinton, Suzette. The Sound of my Life. Purposeful Connections (2013)

Lakota Proverb. https://books.google.co.uk/books?isbn=1462871461

Shaw, George Bernard. (n.d.). BrainyQuote.com. Retrieved April 6, 2016, from BrainyQuote.com Web site: http://www.brainyquote.com/quotes/quotes/g/georgebern109542.html

Phil McGraw. (n.d.). BrainyQuote.com. Retrieved April 30, 2016, from BrainyQuote.com Web site: http://www.brainyquote.com/quotes/quotes/p/philmcgraw204603.html

Henry Wadsworth Longfellow. (n.d.). BrainyQuote.com. Retrieved April 6, 2016, from BrainyQuote.com Web site: http://www.brainyquote.com/quotes/quotes/h/henrywadsw151335.html

Maxwell, Neil A. http://www.azquotes.com/quote/605318

Frankl, Viktor. Man's Search For Meaning. Beacon Press; 1 edition (June 1, 2006)

Chief Seattle. https://books.google.co.uk/books?id=y2UidKLkalgC

Beckwith, Michael. http://www.azquotes.com/quote/669082

Bates, Brian. The Way of Wyrd. Hay House (February 1, 2005)

Tubman, Harriet (n.d.). BrainyQuote.com. Retrieved April 22, 2016, from BrainyQuote.com Web site: http://www.brainyquote.com/quotes/quotes/h/harriettub310306.html

7 Steps to Spiritual Empathy, a Practical Guide

Free Meditation Download.

The Transformational Power of Emotion.

Here are the links to Download both your free Meditation and the Journaling Worksheets that accompany this book.

Download links below

http://www.spiritualempathy.com/meditation/

http://bit.ly/1XkNI53

Jenny also offers readers the opportunity to receive updates about Free Audios and Free Meditations. If this is of interest to you, please register your details on her homepage.

www.jennyflorencehealth.com

A 7 Day Series of Meditations based on this book can be accessed through Jenny's on-line Audio Library.

www.a-z-of-emotionalhealth.com

Made in the USA
Middletown, DE
13 January 2017